DRAWING THE LINE

DRAWING THE LINE

How 31 editors
solved their
toughest
ethical dilemmas

Edited by
Frank McCulloch

Acknowledgements

The idea for this book surfaced at a luncheon for three in St. Petersburg during January 1983. Kay Fanning, chair of ASNE's Ethics Committee, was in town for a seminar at The Poynter Institute for Media Studies. Kay, Gene Patterson and I were talking about ways her committee and our institute might cooperate to expand the dialogue on solving ethical problems in newsrooms. Many ideas were put on the table; one was the unanimous favorite:

Kay's Ethics Committee would ask ASNE members to put in writing the story of a tough ethical dilemma they had faced and how they had resolved it.

The committee would select and edit the best of the anecdotes and meld them into a manuscript.

The Poynter Institute would turn the manuscript into a book and provide a grant to underwrite the cost of publishing it. A copy would be distributed to each ASNE member.

President Creed Black and the ASNE Board approved the idea and it all happened according to plan, because of the special efforts of a few people. Ethics Committee vice chairman Frank McCulloch drew the assignment to edit his fellow editors' stories and decide which ones would be published. His reward in the next life is guaranteed. The introductions to each chapter were written by Dr. Roy Peter Clark, associate director of the Institute. The Afterword, a brief analysis of how editors approach ethical dilemmas based on this group of anecdotes, was written by Dr. Arthur Caplan, a philosopher and ethicist at The Hastings Center, who also has lectured at The Poynter Institute. Copyreading, typesetting and design were supervised by Billie Keirstead, assistant director of the Institute. The cover was designed by Jorge Vargas, a New York artist.

Robert Haiman, President
The Poynter Institute for Media Studies
St. Petersburg, Florida
March 1984

Preface

It's been a worrisome subject since not long after mankind first emerged from caves.

At least as far back as Socrates, the Greeks wrestled with the problem, finally concluding that it couldn't be separated from aesthetics. The Germans took a slightly more ponderous view, seeing it as some sort of ongoing debate between man and God, while the French thought it came down a little closer to a question of whether the wine was properly aged. The British got it all tangled up with the work ethic, and Americans, generally speaking, were too busy conquering a continent to pay it much heed.

That happy heedlessness came to an end with the vanishing of the last frontier. In more recent times, hardly a profession in the land—certainly including journalism—has failed to give increasing attention to two questions: What in the hell is ethics, and once you define it, what do you do about it?

Webster, in answer to the first, says ethics is "the system or code of morals of a particular philosopher, religion, group or profession." That's adequate. The going gets a lot stickier, of course, out beyond the dictionary, out where the real-life decisions grow.

That is precisely what this book is all about: How real-life editors made real-life decisions in painful and complex real-life situations. (Ethics is seldom a problem when complexity and pain are absent.) Their assignment was to describe the toughest ethical decision each had faced, how it was resolved, what the results were, and how the editor now feels about it.

Thirty-one of them did so, and as the reader will find, while common threads are present, 31 of them followed 31 different paths to their decisions.

That is reassuring, for it testifies again to the greatest strength of the free press, which is nothing more than the astonishing degree of individuality among its practitioners. The differences among these stories and the thought processes they represent demonstrate, too, that in journalism, the practice of ethics is inescapably situational. This is the case simply because every situation is so complex and so laden with variables that it is impossible to conceive of anything resembling a common solution. And that in turn is why meaningful and applicable written codes of ethics are so difficult to write, and once written, so frequently violated within hours of being posted on a newsroom wall.

What we have learned as our concern has grown in recent years is that the practice of ethics in journalism is a continuum, a process governed in large part by where on an ever-extending line a particular problem happens to fall.

Some 24 centuries after Socrates had wrapped the Greek worries about ethics into a rational system, another philosopher, George Santayana, observed that Socrates was "hardly proposing practical legislation for mankind (but) merely writing an eloquent epitaph for his country."

There are press haters, I am sure, who will see this book in a similar light. Its real message is something quite removed from such cosmic conclusions. It is simply that the editors who wrote these pieces care very much about what they do, and, perhaps more importantly, care even more about what they do does to others.

Until something better comes along, that will do quite well as a workable definition of ethics.

FRANK McCULLOCH
Executive editor
McClatchy Newspapers.

Contents

Preface
FRANK McCULLOCH/**iv**

I What's a newspaper for anyway?
EUGENE C. PATTERSON
Making choices possible/**3**

DON SHOEMAKER
More than a conduit/**5**

ROBERT M. STIFF
Putting your money where.../**8**

NEIL MORGAN
When the system fails/**10**

II The boundaries of privacy
ROBERT H. PHELPS
An echo of Watergate/**15**

SCOTT McGEHEE
Smaller pieces of life/**18**

ROBERT H. WILLS
A politician's personal life/**22**

WILLIAM B. KETTER
Relevant detail—or needless grief?/**24**

WILLIAM C. HEINE
Damned if we did, damned if we didn't/**26**

ARNOLD ROSENFELD
A dwarf's right to privacy/**28**

III Tough decisions, troubled staff

WILLIAM F. THOMAS
How many believe me now?/**33**

RICHARD H. LEONARD
Young, smart, good—and gone/**35**

KAY FANNING
A rock and a hard place/**37**

THOMAS WINSHIP
Outside work/**40**

FRANK CAPERTON
After the presses roll/**42**

CHARLES C. REYNOLDS
When gambling came to our town/**44**

IV The need for compassion...

STEVE WILSON
It's our pain, too/**49**

WILLIAM BURLEIGH
One city editor's baptism/**51**

ANTHONY E. INSOLIA
Privilege isn't ethics/**53**

ROBERT H. GILES
The Siamese twins case/**55**

DONALD W. GORMLEY
Compassion is a tough word/**58**

RAY MOSCOWITZ
The threat of suicide/**60**

V ...And the need to publish

JOHN STROHMEYER
Keeping good enemies/**65**

DICK SMYSER
Integration in Oak Ridge/**68**

A. N. ROMM
Undercover at Big Nell's/**71**

WILLIAM J. WOESTENDIEK
But isn't football sacred?/**74**

WATSON SIMS
The reality of suicide/**76**

VI When in Rome...

SEYMOUR TOPPING
It was funny, but.../**81**

LOREN GHIGLIONE
Meanwhile, back in Russia.../**83**

VII A case for restraint

ALEX S. JONES
Sticking with named sources/**87**

SUSAN MILLER
Brutal murder, sober restraint/**91**

Afterword

ARTHUR L. CAPLAN
Who ever told you ethics would be easy?/**95**

I   What's a newspaper for anyway?

The philosopher's word for it is *ethos*. It refers to the fundamental values or guiding spirit of a culture or profession. Defining the ethos of a profession inspires insights into how members of that profession should act. What, then, is the ethos of journalism? What's a newspaper for anyway?

American newspapers are not empty vessels which receive the information of the world and pour it out indiscriminately for readers. Newspapers are businesses protected by the Constitution. They make money to do their job, and they do their job to make money. But they also reflect and transmit the values of the system which protects them. They have freedom, power and responsibilities.

The editors herein question how the newspaper should use its power as an institution. How does a newspaper reconcile its business needs with its responsibilities to print important information in a fair and comprehensive way? Should the activities of a newspaper be limited to editorial concerns or does it have legitimate interests as a corporate citizen? Are editors communicators or crusaders? Does freedom of the press belong only to those who can afford one? How do newspapers help give expression to views which run contrary to editorial policy, majority opinion, or both?

Making choices possible

By Eugene C. Patterson

I get mail from some readers who perceive an ethical gulf between our ivory tower and our counting house.

Editorially we warn against the perils of tobacco. Yet we print cigarette advertisements.

We stand foursquare against alcoholism. But we print liquor ads.

We denounce apartheid in South Africa. Still we print that nation's advertisement of Krugerrands, helping to enrich its economy.

We frown on pornography. Yet we publish ads for X-rated movies. (We do limit the size of them and require cleansing of dirtier titles and illustrations, so convict me of practicing situational ethics if you wish.)

We exposed local lawbreaking by a cult called the Church of Scientology. Still, we take advertisements for promotional meetings it conducts.

We advocate handgun control. And we print ads for guns.

The list goes on, and the mail flows in from readers who pronounce us hypocritical and money-grubbers.

They can't see the ads we don't accept, of course—the fraudulent stuff, the libelous, the hurtfully tasteless, the marginally legal, or the pimping, the bait-and-switch merchandising of TV sets which our consumer reporters exposed (we threw out the sharpster's ads and he went out of business.) We do enforce strict advertising standards of acceptability.

But only we can know that. Many readers see enough advertising accepted from sources we've denounced to assume revenue supersedes rectitude on our scale of values. They perceive money as our moral motivator. They do not turn around that assumption and give us credit for having the editorial valor to bite the hand that feeds us. I am convinced, even though

I cannot convince our doubters, that our practice is the ethical one, because...

It's a free country. A newspaper that chooses not to print new or lawful advertising simply because it editorially disagrees with the thrust of the information is, in my judgment, blinding a community to what is going on in its midst. A community so blinded has no basis for deciding whether it approves or disapproves. The newspaper has presumed not simply to recommend standards editorially; it has decided it will enforce its predilections on others by censoring reality.

Some people out there go to X-rated movies, or cult meetings. They drink or smoke or buy guns or Krugerrands. They're free people who have the right to do those things, or not to do them, whether the editor likes it or not. The ethical choice is theirs to make, not his to enforce. A responsible newspaper's duty surely is to illuminate those choices, not to hide them from the people.

EUGENE C. PATTERSON is editor and president of The St. Petersburg (Fla.) Times.

More than a conduit

By Don Shoemaker

It was 70 years ago—in 1913—that the Florida legislature adopted a statute providing that "if any newspaper...assails the personal character of any candidate...or charges said candidate with malfeasance or misfeasance in office or otherwise attacks his official record...such newspaper shall upon request...immediately publish free of cost any reply he may make thereto in as conspicuous a place and in the same kind of type...."

The law (Statute 104.38) gathered dust for 58 years until it was invoked by a disgruntled politician against Editor Herbert Davidson of the *Daytona Beach News-Journal*. Davidson was arrested but quickly freed by a judge who held the statute unconstitutional.

I bumped into the same law two years later in the case which became known as *Pat Tornillo Jr. v The Miami Herald Publishing Company*. Tornillo, head of a teachers' union, was running for the state legislature. We pronounced him undesirable in two editorials before the election, and on the eve of the primary he appeared in my office with a letter we had previously refused to publish and read us Statute 104.38, demanding publication. Once again, we rejected the letter, which defended his candidacy.

Was he denied access to the *Herald?* He was, but for good reasons. He had led a teachers' strike in Florida that closed the schools for 30 days and agonized the state. More importantly, perhaps, he had before then (and has since) written many letters which we published.

I felt this particular one was self-serving and irrelevant, since our readers knew Tornillo and his record well. (He lost the election, as it turned out.) Still, was my denying him the right of reply ethical?

It is a cardinal rule of most editors that readers have responsible access to their pages. The *Herald* has a huge letters section and often publishes letters strongly critical of its policies. But it does so voluntarily and not under duress.

As I saw it, what had altered the case was the threatened employment of Statute 104.38, which we knew to be unconstitutional from the *Davidson* case and which, the day after, was held void for the same reasons in Dade County court when Tornillo sought to have me arrested.

I think that Tom Wicker in the *New York Times* summed it up pretty well: "It may well be that Florida voters would have been better served had the *Herald* printed Mr. Tornillo's reply. Even so, this is a specific case. It is highly doubtful that a law like Florida's, if held constitutional and applied by all the states, would serve the public's need to know and the principle of fairness. It would more likely lead editors to refrain from publishing critical investigative or controversial material, knowing that to do so would lead to the necessity for printing replies, whether justified or not."

Our own editorial said that "we believe that the newspaper's editor should be the judge of what it prints—not the government." If I felt any ethical twinge of conscience, I do not remember it. All I remember is the outrage—the pointed gun.

The law provided criminal penalties, and I was far from comfortable when the Florida Supreme Court, with which the *Herald* had long been feuding, upheld it in a 6-1 decision that I editorially called "full of sectional bias and narrow parochialism."

The case went on appeal to the U.S. Supreme Court. Several dozen newspapers and professional organizations joined the *Herald*, sensing that this was a landmark test of the First Amendment. The court agreed with all of us. In a 9-0 opinion, Chief Justice Berger held on June 24, 1974:

"A newspaper is more than a passive receptacle or conduit for news, comment, and advertising. The choice of material to go into a newspaper, and the decisions made as to limitations on the size of the newspaper, and content, and treatment of public issues and public officials—whether fair or unfair—constitute the exercise of editorial control and judgment. It has yet to be demonstrated how government regulation of this crucial process can be exercised consistent with First Amendment guarantees of a free press as they have evolved to this time."

In 1975 the state legislature repealed Statute 104.38.

DON SHOEMAKER is editor emeritus of The Miami (Fla.) Herald.

Putting your money where...

By Robert M. Stiff

My toughest ethical dilemma had nothing to do with a news story. It involved a donation of money by my newspaper company. While it is not unusual for newspapers to give funds to good causes, this was for a political cause. This is the background:

Enough Florida voters signed petitions in 1978 to force a statewide November referendum on changing the state constitution so casino gambling could be legalized.

A little more than two months before the voters would decide this issue, it appeared the pro-casino forces might win. They had raised $3 million, mostly from gambling and hotel interests in places like Las Vegas and Atlantic City. Their media blitz was impressive.

It was also frightening for the lies, misrepresentations and half-truths in their newspaper ads and TV and radio commercials.

Every major daily newspaper that took an editorial stand opposed casino gambling as being harmful to the future of Florida.

Then-Gov. Reubin Askew formed a group called No Casinos Inc. to battle the big money casino supporters. He stumped the state, putting his popularity and political future on the line. But his efforts required money, and he turned to the business community for assistance.

The Times Publishing Co. was one of those asked to help. The motion at our board of directors meeting was to donate $25,000 of corporate funds to help combat the pro-casino forces' advertising blitz.

I wrestled with my conscience for a short time and voted for the motion. I would do it again—for an issue of this importance, but never for a candidate.

I knew the casino people would scream that they could not get fair news coverage because of our financial involvement. But we would have faced that charge without the donation. My newspaper had written dozens of strong anti-casino editorials over the years. The fact that we put our money where our editorial mouths had been wouldn't change the bias charge of opponents.

And I was aware that our company's future was certain to be affected by what kind of state Florida was to become. The business side of our newspaper has an absolute right to meet its corporate responsibility as a good citizen and do what it can to defeat a threat to the state's future economic health. Business success is necessary if we are to fulfill our First Amendment responsibilities and our community obligations.

The voters of Florida deserved to be able to make a well-informed decision in the casino referendum. With one side having $3 million to spend to influence them, I think the $150,000 raised by the state's major newspapers brought a measure of fairness to the issue. Voters got messages from both sides through identical media. In New Jersey, two years earlier, the casinos spent $1.3 million to get a favorable vote. Anti-casino forces were able to raise only $23,000.

Newspaper staffs and readers were informed openly of our financial decision, of course. And the voters turned down casinos by nearly a 3-1 margin.

I was chairman of the ASNE Ethics Committee at the time this occurred, so I was quite conscious of the ethical considerations in this decision. But, given the atmosphere in Florida at that moment, I thought my stance and vote were ethically proper. I still do.

ROBERT M. STIFF is editor of The St. Petersburg (Fla.) Evening Independent.

9

When the system fails

By Neil Morgan

The problem involved a judge, Lewis A. Wenzell, who was 40 years old when he was convicted of soliciting prostitution in 1982. The lurid testimony of prostitutes presented editorial questions of propriety and taste not faced before. Most of the testimony remained unprinted, but community indignation grew as his peers refused to assign cases to him, and he refused to resign.

We began working our way through the ethical dilemma in a conventional position: The jurist's private life was of no great concern, and in most circumstances, certainly no justification for his removal from the bench.

Even after his conviction on five misdeameanor counts, I continued to feel compassion for an obviously troubled man.

But when it became clear that the judicial system itself was either unable or unwilling to discipline one of its own, and that our readers were unwilling to accept that as a final verdict, we decided we faced a greater responsibility.

We called editorially on the California Commission on Judicial Performance to act on the case and urged our readers to communicate with members of the Commission, which moved with rare speed both to bar the judge from hearing cases and to rule that he was guilty of moral turpitude. His attorney challenged this; the California Supreme Court became the court of next resort for the judge's civil case as his attorney pursued his criminal appeal in lower courts. Then an appellate court in an adjacent county reversed the judge's conviction by a vote of 2-to-1 on grounds of judicial error: The trial judge had spoken to jurors outside the hearing of attorneys.

With hundreds of readers telephoning protests concerning the lack of movement in the case, we checked with election officials, the district attorney, our own attorneys, and decided to reprint a recall petition that had been circulated unsuccessfully many weeks earlier. We printed our corporate postal frank on the reverse side of the ballot, making it a clip-and-mail. It appeared in the *Tribune* on three days, along with editorials explaining our action. In a staff meeting before the first publication, we discussed the action, saying that what we were doing was perhaps unique, but that the Wenzell case itself was unusual, and that this was an opportunity for two-way communication with our readers on a local issue that had inflamed the city.

Some were concerned that the newspaper was involving itself too deeply. Others argued that this was the kind of action that only newspapers can lead. The action was supported by 95 percent of those who wrote letters to the editor, although a protest from the American Civil Liberties Union held that ours was an unprecedented and unfair deployment of the power of the press.

Eventually, about 30,000 signatures were returned to the newspaper and passed on to the authorities. The judge then resigned with a bitter blast at the *Tribune.* Despite that, the recall petition qualified for the ballot, and, although the issue was moot, voters confirmed his resignation by the largest recall majority in California history.

In the months of second-guessing that followed our action and the judge's resignation, I came to a firm conclusion: Readers properly expect their newspaper editors to stand and take sides. In the end, that seems to me to be our duty.

NEIL MORGAN is editor of The San Diego (Calif.) Tribune.

II The boundaries of privacy

The most difficult ethical decisions for journalists involve not the conflict between good and evil but the resolution of conflicting goods. It is good to publish information that readers may find useful or interesting. It is also good to protect the privacy of individuals. Sometimes it may be impossible to do both.

Do even the most public figures, in the most important stories, have parts of their lives which should be protected from public disclosure? Do some news sources, especially the naive or inexperienced, deserve special protection from the consequences of appearing in print?

The editors in this section consider the boundaries of privacy in stories involving individuals as diverse as an American president, a stage mother, a local politician, the son of a criminal, a victim of rape and a dwarf.

Their questions and second thoughts center on the tension between disclosure and privacy, between the public's right to know and its need to know.

An echo of Watergate

By Robert H. Phelps

It was Satchel Paige, who pitched in the major leagues until he was an old man, who sounded the warning: "Don't look back; something might be gaining on you."

Generally I have followed Satch's advice. I have not anguished over decisions made as an editor for very long after the paper went to bed, whether that paper was the *New York Times* or the *Boston Globe.*

There was one decision I made, however, that years later still bothers me. It was an ethical lapse that haunts me even though the victim was a man I did not admire, Richard M. Nixon.

Here was the situation: It was March 26, 1976. At that time I was managing editor of the *Boston Globe* and therefore responsible for putting out the morning paper. Late in the day *Newsweek* released in Washington excerpts from the book, *Final Days,* by Bob Woodward and Carl Bernstein, the *Washington Post* reporters who had outdistanced everyone else in covering the Watergate scandal.

The story by the *Globe's* Washington Bureau led with Nixon's praying hysterically with Secretary of State Henry Kissinger the night before the President resigned. Other juicy details followed: Nixon's weeping, his drinking, his family's worry that he might kill himself. On and on.

It was a good story because it revealed so many things about the crumbling Presidency. There was no question that it would go on page one. I read deep into the copy, wallowing in the disclosures. Then I came to this paragraph:

"The President became increasing isolated from his family. Mrs. Pat Nixon, the book reports, wanted a divorce in 1962 when Nixon ran unsuccessfully for governor of California. According to one excerpt recounted by *New York Daily News* columnist Liz Smith, Mrs. Nixon confided to someone in the White House physician's office that she and the President had not had sexual relations for 14 years."

That last sentence disturbed me. I had only a little problem with running the report on Mrs. Nixon's desire for a divorce. Yes, it was personal and, yes, spouses sometimes do express such thoughts in the heat of anger without ever really intending to go through with them. But, like many other politicians, Nixon had used his wife in campaigning; therefore, their relationship was fair game for public reporting.

The sexual relationship gave me more pause. Wasn't that going too far? I asked a number of other editors whether we should kill the passage. The response (of course there were predictable bad jokes) was divided, but I believe most of the editors favored printing the entire passage. I still hesitated. There was the question of trusting the authors. Woodward and Bernstein had proved right on Watergate when seasoned reporters, including some of the best on the *Washington Post,* had insisted they were wrong.

I do not remember questioning the odd attribution of the sentence on the sexual relationship to Liz Smith, the gossip columnist. Actually the Smith report on the book went too far. The Woodward-Bernstein book said this regarding Mrs. Nixon's relationship with the President: "She and her husband had not really been close since the early 1960s, the First Lady confided to one of her White House physicians. She had wanted to divorce him after his 1962 defeat in the California gubernatorial campaign. She tried, and failed, to win his promise not to seek office again. Her rejection of his advances since then had seemed to shut something off inside Nixon. But they had stuck it out."

Eventually I decided to let the sentence run. Never before had we had a Presidential resignation. Any light that could be shed on that Presidency, that could offer clues to the failure of the man as a leader, was justified.

The next day, on reading the story in print, I realized that I had made a serious mistake. I had let my feelings about the evils of the Nixon Presidency override professional ethical standards that should protect the privacy of every individual whether good or evil. The relationship between the Nixons was based on sheer rumor. In the case of the sexual relationship, the report had come not directly from the *Newsweek* excerpts but from what a gossip columnist had heard about the excerpts. There was no evidence to support the statement, no evidence that even if true, the absence of a sexual relationship had an effect on Nixon as a key Watergate figure or as President. I'm sorry I let that passage stand.

ROBERT H. PHELPS is vice president of Affiliated Publications and is the former executive editor of The Boston (Mass.) Globe.

Smaller pieces of life

By Scott McGehee

The most difficult ethical questions, in my view, are not always the momentous ones. When the issues are large—whether to publish leaks from a grand jury about an investigation of public wrongdoing or whether to use two days beforehand information that could affect the outcome of an election—the questions are clear and the answers are more likely to present themselves with equal clarity.

When the issues are the smaller pieces of everyday life, the questions may never get asked. If the questions are raised, the answers often are murky.

In two stories, one published and one withheld, hindsight convinces me I made one wrong decision and one right one. The right one was not to publish the story, and that goes against all our instincts in the news business. There is the danger.

Both stories involve the more or less private lives of ordinary people, not usually subjects of news stories.

The first was the lead story in a Sunday lifestyle section, a profile of a tennis mother, thoroughly researched, beautifully written—and devastating.

The reporter had spent occasional whole days for weeks with the mother and her talented, preteen, tennis-playing son. The mother had opened up—sometimes in post-midnight telephone calls to the reporter—to reveal her innermost hopes, dreams and fears. The reporter, a former tennis prodigy herself, had taken it all in.

The resulting story painted in vivid detail the sad case of a mother living through her son, single minded in her devotion to his success, suffocating in the pressure she applied. The story of this one woman and her son was skillfully constructed to illustrate the stage-mother, little-league-father syndrome, with lessons to be inferred by any caring parent.

18

When I first read the story, I couldn't believe the mother had been so willing to allow herself to look so bad. I challenged the reporter on how she had gotten much of the information: Did the mother know from the beginning that she was talking to a reporter working on a story? Was each quote exactly accurate and in context? How could the reporter know this or that intimate detail? I was satisfied with the answers, and although I knew the mother and her friends and family would not be happy with the portrait it painted, I wanted to see that story in the newspaper. I knew it would be read and talked about. It was a very good story.

Several days after publication, I got a telephone call from a woman with a quavering voice who said she was that mother. She had already talked to her lawyer, who had convinced her she couldn't get successful legal revenge. But she wanted me to know that the reporter and I had ruined her marriage, her relationship with her son, her life. She had bared her soul to the reporter, who had used it as grist for a mean, unfair story, she said.

That was all: one phone call. No face-to-face confrontation, no barrage of complaints from friends and family, no spate of canceled subscriptions, no lawsuit filed. But the pain in the woman's voice still haunts me.

So do the questions I didn't ask: Did the reporter have some unresolved problems from her own tennis-playing youth that colored the story unfairly? Would the story have worked just as well without the mean tone? Did the reporter get too close, allowing the mother to assume she was a friend, not merely a reporter? Did the story unfairly take advantage of a woman who had no previous experience dealing with the press?

I'll never know the answer to most of those questions, but I know the answer to the last one: Yes.

The second story was one of 46 capsule case histories running with a six-part series. After a controversial case, two reporters spent months examining all 199 sentences given for manslaughter in Michigan in 1982. To humanize and illustrate this massive look at how part of the criminal justice system works, the case histories provided easy reading and gripping detail. Most involved knifings, shootings, beatings and drunk driving.

One involved a 19-year-old college student who told her family she was suffering from a "water bubble" on her stomach. She closed herself in her bedroom one day, gave birth to a baby which she wrapped in a sweater and put in the closet, and then got in the shower. Her parents found blood on the bedclothes and rushed her to the hospital, where they were told they should return home and look for a baby. The baby was dead.

The woman's brother found out we were going to include his sister's case in our story. He pleaded with me not to use her name. He said she was coming through two years of psychiatric treatment, was back in school and had just become engaged to be married. Dredging up the case in the newspaper would ruin her life, he said.

He said her case had been handled through a youthful offenders program which was supposed to suppress all the records. We had gotten them, through no special effort, with the 198 others.

When I raised the brother's concern with the editor and reporters on the story, they were sympathetic. No one likes the prospect of ruining someone's life. But they argued we needed to use names with all the case histories for the sake of authenticity; they argued we were using cases involving younger people (and she was legally an adult); they argued others among the 46 could complain—and some had—that rehashing their cases in the newspaper would damage their lives, too. And they argued a baby had died, after all, and in virtually all the cases it was an irrational act that led to tragedy.

I worried about treating all 46 with evenhandedness. I agreed with the reporters that it might not be fair to exclude just this case. But in the end, my not entirely rational decision—based on the feeling in my stomach as much as anything—was to omit that young woman's story. In a gesture toward evenhandedness, we omitted the one other case history involving the same youthful offenders program. The series worked just fine without them.

SCOTT McGEHEE is the managing editor of The Detroit (Mich.) Free Press

A politician's personal life

By Robert H. Wills

When does the private behavior of a public official become news? When does an editor have an obligation to tell his readers about a politician's unsavory personal life?

The editors of the *Milwaukee Sentinel* wrestled with these questions in 1972 as they considered information on the activities of County Supervisor Richard C. Nowakowski.

Nowakowski, 39, a colorful politician, had long attracted attention with his flamboyant tactics. He enjoyed the limelight and relished the trappings of office. He was mentioned frequently as ambitious for higher office.

In 1972 he defeated a courthouse veteran in a fight for the county board chairmanship, a powerful position. From that point on, the rumors about Nowakowski's questionable activities—some of them involving his political life—intensified and could no longer be ignored.

A team of *Sentinel* reporters set out to find answers to the question: What kind of man holds this influential post?

Their findings included some activities in both his public and private life that appeared to be questionable, including campaign laws violations and his involvement in swinging parties. The reporters also learned of Nowakowski's longstanding illicit relationship with a woman.

The question then became whether the *Sentinel* should make public the knowledge it had about Nowakowski, even though he had not been accused in criminal complaints, or his ethics challenged, and if so, should the seamy details of his private life be aired along with his public misdeeds?

Should the newspaper initiate the subjects for the community?

The decision was made at a meeting of the editor of the *Sentinel,* who was also a vice president; the managing editor; the city editor, and the chairman of the board.

We obtained advice from outside legal counsel, discussed the legal risks and the ethical questions. Finally, we decided to go ahead with the stories.

Our reasoning? We believed that we had the responsibility to let the community know of the personal background, the character and the activities of this elected official. We were certain that the judgment he used in his personal life would be the same kind of judgment he would use in his governmental decision-making, and we were equally certain that an enlightened citizenry would reach the same conclusion.

Our stories set off a furor. There were investigations by state and federal authorities and, eventually, grand jury indictments. Nowakowski was indicted on eight felony counts.

In 1974, a jury acquitted Nowakowski of a charge of accepting a bribe. Five counts of soliciting perjury were dismissed, but he was subsequently convicted of violating the state's Corrupt Practices Act and fined $1,000 for accepting $800 in postage stamps as part of a campaign contribution.

The felony conviction automatically removed Nowakowski from office. His political career was over. His marriage ended in 1977. He moved to Florida and died there of a heart attack on June 12, 1982.

At the time of the 1972 stories, the *Sentinel* was both praised and criticized for bringing Nowakowski's activities to light; the criticism was mainly over whether the unsavory details of his personal life should have been publicized.

In retrospect, we are convinced that the decision made that day by *Sentinel* editors and executives was the right one. If we had to do it over, we would do it again.

ROBERT H. WILLS is the editor of The Milwaukee (Wis.) Sentinel.

23

Relevant detail— or needless grief?

By William B. Ketter

The first three paragraphs of the front-page story told how carbon monoxide fumes from a faulty automobile exhaust had killed a young man and left his girl friend seriously ill while they were parked with the car engine idling.

In the next two paragraphs, the story identified the victim as the son of a convicted organized crime figure who was prominently in the news before he was sent off to federal prison. The final eight paragraphs dealt with information about the accident and the young people involved.

It was the details about the father's notorious past that so disturbed a number of our readers. They questioned why we would even mention it when the story was about the son's unfortunate death, not about the father.

"It wasn't pertinent at all," said one reader. "It was embarrassing information that should not have been printed."

Why did we publish it?

Our answer is not one everybody can understand or accept, but we simply concluded that the father's background was relevant because of who he was. We would have reached the same decision had the story involved any other person who had achieved prominence or notoriety.

This background, by the way, affected the investigation of the accident. Police considered a possible gangland connection, but determined there was none.

The should we/shouldn't we dilemma always will haunt us because there is no clear line to draw. While some readers may regard making the kind of connection we did as both unnecessary and insensitive, others would consider this a serious sin of omission for there is a public perception that newspapers deliberately refuse to publish certain controversial details. As such critics see it, what gets in and what's left out relate somehow to money and power, and this, of course, goes straight to a paper's credibility.

For all of that, in the minds of many readers we had changed the focus of the story from an account of a tragedy to one that caused further needless grief. As so often happens, we saw ourselves driven by good intentions, while readers saw us as interested only in selling newspapers.

Newspapers obviously are not always right and are not always compassionate. But one thing is certain: We are always burdened by the very real consequences of our decisions.

WILLIAM B. KETTER is editor of The Quincy (Mass.) Patriot-Ledger.

Damned if we did, damned if we didn't

By William C. Heine

When a firm ethical policy is broken, even unintentionally, the resulting problems are unusually difficult to resolve.

Near London a few years ago, two men broke into the home of the manager of a jewelry manufacturing plant. One held the wife and a child hostage in a bedroom while the other took the husband to open the plant and the safe. The two men escaped with considerable loot.

The *London Free Press* carried the story, naming the firm, the husband and wife and the usual other details.

Some time later, two men were arrested and tried. During the trial, there was testimony concerning a woman having been forced to have oral sex with the man holding her hostage. The reporter included the detail in an account of the trial, being careful not to name the woman. Under a long-established policy, the *London Free Press* does not identify the victim in rape cases.

What no one recalled or considered was that the woman had been named in the original story about the hostage-taking and the robbery.

It soon came to me that we had inadvertently identified the rape victim to all those who knew about the hostages—in effect, just about everyone in the community.

A relative of the family bitterly complained and demanded that we do something to remedy our error.

I was fully prepared to apologize both in person and in the newspaper. The problem was if I did so in the newspaper, we would once again bring the matter to the attention of readers who knew the woman.

In a misguided effort to placate understandably distressed people, I sent a memo to the newsroom banning the use of the phrase "oral sex" under any circumstances. That stood for several months until a more rational colleague pointed out there were legitimate medical and other news stories referring to oral sex. So I lifted that ban.

Still in effect, however, is a strong admonition to copy editors to make quite certain that there is no reference, direct or indirect, which could lead to public identification of a rape victim.

In our last conversation, the victim's relative and I agreed there was nothing more we could do. Long prison terms for both men had helped the victim adjust to her experience. In time, her memories faded, as did those of others in the community.

For me, it was a deeply frustrating experience. I could neither defend the newspaper's right to publish information the public was entitled to know, nor publish our apologies for what the victim would always see as a grievous error on our part.

WILLIAM G. HEINE is editor of The London (Ontario) Free Press.

A dwarf's right to privacy

By Arnold Rosenfeld

What are the rights to privacy of a person who is a dwarf? I was managing editor of the *Dayton Daily News* when that troubling question reached me. The first thing I heard was that our Lifestyle department had a terrific section front story for Sunday. The story, it was reported to me with great enthusiasm, concerned a special class run by the Dayton public schools for youngsters with severe deformities.

It was a sensitive story, sensitively reported. We had been invited to report it by the class and its instructor, all of whom wanted to demonstrate what each person had done to overcome a clearly enormous handicap. Our reporter found that a young woman, 17, who was a dwarf, had emerged as class leader. It was her courage, spirit and energy that had literally propelled this class of brave youngsters. Let's call her Mary.

Given the sensitivity of the story, I asked a few questions about how we had obtained it. I was assured that each person involved was not only aware that there was to be a story, but was enormously enthusiastic about it.

We had taken photographs to accompany the story. I asked to see them. They were excellent pictures—honest but not grotesque. I asked to see the entire layout when it was completed.

The next thing I heard, perhaps the following day, was that the parents of Mary, the young class leader, had objected violently to the story. A few minutes later, Mary's father called. He was not just upset, he was abusive. He threatened suit. He insisted his family's privacy was being violated. He would not be placated.

I told him that we had received permission, including his daughter's, to do the story. He replied that his permission had not been solicited—or received. I said we felt the story would do a great deal of good, and that it showed his daughter in the best possible light, demonstrating her courage, her positive personality, her capacity for leadership. He said he didn't care. I asked him if killing the story didn't undermine the very point of what his family had accomplished with this young woman. He said that wasn't any of my business, that this was a situation he had had to live with, not I. I asked if I could talk to Mary. He refused. She was too upset, he said.

The conversation ended angrily. He continued to demand that I kill the story, or at least remove his daughter and her pictures. I, in turn, insisted it was a significant story to which we had a perfect right. Publicly, I defended journalism. Privately, I was deeply disturbed.

I had a day or so to think about it. In the end, I took a middle ground. Mary, her story and pictures, were removed from the copy. My Lifestyle editor, her reporter and the photographer were miserably unhappy. The project ran in its now truncated form, severely damaged, I had to admit. It was not a great day for journalism.

But I still feel good about the decision. People who are dwarfs, I decided, have greater claims concerning privacy than most. Their objections, particularly in the softer news area, must carry almost ultimate weight with us.

This story counts for almost nothing in its narrowest sense. It is important journalistically, I think, only because it proves that the search for an all-purpose, one-size-fits-all ethical code will inevitably be frustrated. Everybody is searching for such rules, a statement for which this book is best evidence.

The decisions straight out of the book are easy. It is, unfortunately, the two or three percent for which there are no book rules that we earn our pay—and reputations.

Newspaper journalism pretty obviously has the capacity for great good and great damage, occasionally both at the same time. Unfortunately, the ethics of journalism and the ethics of the real world do not always mesh. In these cases, I think we ought to think seriously about giving the real world a couple of extra percentage points in the decision making process, for I have found that we are too often at our most gutless when we think we are being the most bravely journalistic.

Rules or ethics do not free us from our responsibilities to understand and share some of the human pain that sometimes grows out of our decision to publish.

ARNOLD ROSENFELD is editor of The Dayton (Ohio) Daily News and Journal Herald.

III Tough decisions, troubled staff

Editors lead their newspapers by policy, by direction and by example. They communicate their values to the staff through hiring and firing, budget control and decisions about story play. It has been said that a newspaper takes on the personality of its top editor.

A newspaper staff expects much from an editor, including an occasional walk on water. Reporters expect editors to be courageous and independent. They want editors to spend money to achieve editorial excellence. Reporters can become disillusioned or cynical when an editor shows favoritism toward friends or benefactors, or when an editor tries to rein in an aggressive reporting team, or when an editor permits a newspaper to be embarrassed by the competition. An editor can make a tough decision, even the right tough decision, and be left with a troubled or angry staff.

Because journalists are storytellers and gossip mongers, anecdotes about senior editorial behavior are saved and passed on from reporter to reporter, sometimes for generations. For better or worse, they become the parables which shape the behavior of journalists.

How many believe me now?

By William F. Thomas

The ethical decisions that appear difficult, in my experience, rarely are. Troublesome, yes, but not all that tough to call.

Among these, I include a story on the California Supreme Court which we ran on the day of a state election to recall Chief Justice Rose Bird. She didn't look good in the story, and she only barely beat the recall.

No editor would run such a story at this crucial time unless it clearly was relevant and unless its central elements had been verified and every chance had been offered for rebuttal. I was satisfied then and I remain satisfied today that the story met these tests, but we're still seeing published criticism, more righteous than informed, about a decision which I regarded as unavoidable.

In a different category, and far more difficult in my view, are those decisions which require an editor to overrule his staff under circumstances which could call his motivations into question.

These calls are always close. There are valid arguments on both sides that rarely involve issues important to anyone but yourself, those staff members involved and the subject of the story.

A recent illustration: A story about the son of a long-time political figure quoted, in the midst of a long and free-wheeling interview, an ambiguous reference by him to Hitler. The context involved some fanciful musings on medical experiments on humans, so you can see the possibilities here.

I was on vacation when I was called by the father of this young fellow, himself an elected official. The father was overwrought. He pleaded for what he saw as his son's political future. He said his son would be destroyed politically by his admittedly stupid reference to Hitler.

I found on my return to the office that the father and the son had called the reporter more than once, cajoling at first and then threatening. The threat referred, or was presumed by the reporter and her superiors to refer, to the father's influence with, among others, myself and the publisher.

I need not say that at this point I hoped very much that the story would stand up.

There followed more phone calls to me and one to the publisher, who was mystified and wisely chose to remain so. I then read the story, and came to the melancholy conclusions that: 1) the reference to Hitler was more puzzling than relevant; 2) it had no bearing whatever on the thrust of the story, which mainly portrayed the father's determination to shape a political future for his not-so-sharp son, and 3) the son, apprised of what he'd said, declared that, for God's sake, he didn't mean he agreed with that monster about anything.

Further, there was little doubt in my mind, or anyone else's, that the quote, however ambiguous, would be very damaging to his political future.

The department editor, the reporter's bureau chief and the reporter each felt that the quote, while troublesome to them, showed how this fellow's mind worked and, in an exhaustive profile such as this, was legitimate.

I had no doubt that the quote was accurate, but I felt that its use—especially when it was disavowed—was overkill. Any reference to Hitler carried with it such emotional baggage that it must be used, unless it is clearly condemnatory, only with great care. Such, at any rate, was my thinking.

So I talked with the reporter and the two editors and then killed the Hitler reference. Then I fired off a letter to the father, saying in effect that I had edited the story for the reasons I've outlined here, but that his asinine behavior, far from inspiring this action, had made it extremely difficult.

And now, I can only wonder how many believe me.

WILLIAM F. THOMAS is editor and executive vice president of The Los Angeles (Calif.) Times.

34

Young, smart, good— and gone

By Richard H. Leonard

The new investigative reporter was a whiz. Young, smart, good appearance, tough but not abrasive, good writer, upward bound. He had done well on several assignments and was ready for a big one.

There were rumors that a major bank holding company was in trouble. Find out, he was told, if the rumors are true and just how bad the trouble is.

Writing about banks in trouble is a delicate matter requiring skill in obtaining information and sound judgment in how the material is presented. We felt he could handle it.

Our investigator went to work, writing cautiously and objectively about the bank holding company's finances, letting the facts speak for themselves.

Trading in the holding company stock was suspended by the Wisconsin Securities Commissioner. A key story was the *Journal's* report that the company had lost $15.4 million in the current year.

The story was hot.

Then, to our horror, we read in another newspaper that our man on the assignment was the high bidder for 6,060 shares of the holding company stock. He had bid 22 cents a share at an auction for stock with a par value of $5 and a book value of $7.50, expecting the price to rise when trading resumed.

There we were. Our talented, objective reporter was now a stockholder in the distressed company whose plight he had helped to reveal.

Conflict of interest?

No, our investigator said. The stock auction had been advertised in the paper and he had not used inside information. Anybody could have made a bid. It was all legal. It was a legitimate investment based on knowledge available to anyone who read the paper.

Did he think he could continue to cover the bank story in an objective way?

Of course, he said. Nobody could buy him. He had turned down people who had offered him free trips, jobs and money.

What about the public's perception of the objectivity of a story written by one of the holding company's own stockholders?

No problem there, he said.

"Sell the stock by 3 p.m. today and report back when you've done it," we replied.

At 3 p.m. he returned to announce that he had decided not to sell.

"You're fired," we said. He sighed and left.

Then we wrote a short note explaining to the staff that the reporter had been terminated for failing to meet the *Journal's* standards of reporting. The note was put on the bulletin board and we awaited staff reaction. Would they take the position that his investment was none of our business? Would they agree with him that he didn't have a conflict of interest?

I sat at my desk prepared to argue with anyone who wanted to argue. A reporter stuck his head in the door.

"You did the right thing," he said. Others came over to concur. One staffer was quoted in *Columbia Journalism Review* as saying, as I recall it, "You could practically hear cheering in the city room."

It was a great afternoon for believers in ethical reporting.

RICHARD H. LEONARD is editor of The Milwaukee (Wis.) Journal.

A rock and a hard place

By Kay Fanning

The disconsolate banker was waiting when I returned to the paper after dinner.

I knew why he was there. He had just learned that the *Daily News* was preparing to write a story about his son, who was under investigation for arson. The midnight torching and total destruction of the popular Bobby McGee's Restaurant had shocked the city. Now the revelation that the suspected arsonist was the wealthy son of one of Anchorage's most respected families—and himself the owner of a competing restaurant—would stun the community.

We had known for six months about the investigation that implicated Frank Reed Jr. Reporter Don Hunter brought in regular reports from confidential sources, but we remained silent while the probe continued, hoping we could verify independently what we were hearing. Now, our sources told us, a grand jury indictment was imminent. We had just learned that the U.S. attorney had sent a letter to Reed advising him that he was the target of an investigation. We had also discovered that the authorities had incriminating tape recordings. Yet no source would speak for attribution, and we didn't have a copy of the U.S. attorney's letter or any other document.

The key editors were ready to publish. "Why now?" I asked.

"Because it's 'on the street.' The competition may have it soon." We had countless hours invested in the story.

Against this backdrop, Frank Reed Sr. had come to say his son had been framed, that he was sure there would be no indictment. If we published now and there was no indictment, we would ruin his son's life, damage his small children, wreck the family.

As I faced the agonized father, my thoughts raced to the time when Frank Reed Sr., one of Anchorage's most prominent civic leaders, had been the only member of the business community who had publicly supported my newspaper during a desperate period of financial instability and conflict with the competing newspaper. He had cochaired a committee whose work helped keep the *Anchorage Daily News* alive. Now he was begging me not to run the story about his son.

Most of the time I had a pretty good rapport with the newsroom staff. Tonight they were waiting to see what I would do—whether I would be swayed by the wealthy banker's clout. The executive editor was adamant: We should publish in tomorrow morning's paper.

"Why can't we wait until the indictment comes down?" I asked.

"Because we've been sitting on the story for months. We have it confirmed by several sources. And if we don't publish, the competition will."

"What if the man has been framed?"

"Everything indicates he's guilty as hell."

"What's the harm to the public interest in waiting a few days to see?" I also asked if we could get any official to go on the record. "No."

The story would be attributed only to *"Daily News* sources." We would be asking our readers to trust us that it was true.

As I tussled with the problem, I felt certain any respect the newsroom and my executive editor might have for me would vanish if I "caved in." In 15 years working together, he and I had never had a confrontation like this.

I turned to reporter Don Hunter. "Why do you think we should run the story now?" I asked.

He hesitated. "I'm not sure. It's on the street."

A decision could be delayed no longer. "Hold the story," I said, reversing the executive editor. Daggers.

My reasoning was simple: Was beating the competition enough reason to risk damaging someone's life and reputation? What public interest was really being served by printing this story before the indictment? It was bad luck that everyone knew I was emotionally indebted to Frank Reed Sr., but that was irrelevant to the principle involved.

Would I have made the same decision if the father had been an unknown? I certainly hope so. Would I have taken so much heat? No.

A week later Frank Reed Jr. was indicted for arson. This time, my luck was good. We got the story first.

KAY FANNING is editor of The Christian Science Monitor. She was formerly editor and publisher of The Anchorage (Alaska) Daily News.

Outside work

By Thomas Winship

One of the most complicated and still-evolving areas of ethics is that of activities outside the paper by news personnel. The question is simply to what extent reporters, editors and photographers should be limited in their non-newspaper activities.

The latest incident in this evolution at the *Globe* occurred early in 1983, when a photographer asked for permission to take pictures for the Boston Red Sox. The pictures were to be used for such promotional purposes as yearbooks, programs and posters.

Until the recent past, it was not unusual for photographers to moonlight for sports teams and racetracks. But as newspapers have come to realize, their strength depends heavily on the impartiality that they can bring to the coverage of any subject, whether it be sports, business, government or fashion.

The *Globe* denied the request, taking the position that it cannot have any of its news staff working for a major newsmaking organization that it covers regularly. Outside activities are covered by our union/management contract, so the matter ended up in arbitration.

The *Globe* argued that to have its news staffers associated directly with newsmakers undermines the integrity and credibility of the newspaper—that once it became known a news staffer was working for the Red Sox, the public would begin to lose confidence in the impartiality of the *Globe's* coverage.

Furthermore, the loyalty of the individual involved would be split. As an example, in 1982 a young boy sitting near the first-base dugout in Fenway Park was hit in the head by a line drive foul. He was handed down a couple of rows of seats and in a very dramatic scene was carried from the field to the clubhouse by Red Sox star Jim Rice.

If assigned to the game, would a photographer who also worked for the public relations arm of the Red Sox take a picture of the serious injury of a small boy, even if it were dramatic and involved a major star? If he were not to be assigned to the Red Sox, were we giving up assignment flexibility we should not have to?

We were successful in convincing the arbitrator that the ethical questions that we raised at a formal hearing were founded in very basic practical matters and that the contract supported our position.

The Red Sox case has cleared the air, at least at the *Globe* and at least for the time being.

THOMAS WINSHIP is the editor of The Boston (Mass.) Globe.

After the presses roll

By Frank Caperton

The ethical decisions I dread most as an editor involve cases in which the presses have already rolled—and we have published a story that is fundamentally unfair.

My difficulty with these discipline situations flows from the fact I'm not an absolutist. Not even every serious breech of professional ethics is necessarily a firing offense.

The factors I try to consider include the severity of the offense, the amount of damage it does and the experience and post-event attitude of the staffers. Inevitably, I also find myself making a best-judgment decision about basic character.

Consider a specific case:

A local tourist attraction had run a highly visible multi-media ad campaign touting its wares. Two young members of our staff—one the editor of a zoned edition, the other a staff writer in another department—became paying customers of the attraction. They felt the attraction had not lived up to its billing and provided poor service.

The two collaborated on a letter to the editor, signed with fictitious names, that noted how severely the actual experience had fallen short of that advertised. The editor then published the letter in his zoned edition.

Both staffers could have been fired. That option was given serious consideration, but finally rejected. The steps the managing editor and I took involved:

• A personal apology from the managing editor to the management of the attraction.

• A correction and apology published in the zoned edition in which the letter appeared.

• A two-week suspension without pay and formal letter of reprimand for the editor.

- A one-week suspension without pay and formal letter of reprimand for the writer.

The managing editor explained to both staff members there would be no further chances if they committed another action that raised questions about their honesty.

The managing editor and I decided against firing based on our judgment—supported by the staffers' immediate supervisors—that though this had been a stupid, thoughtless act, it was not typical of either one's character.

The incident took place several years ago. Both writer and editor are still productive news professionals.

In another case, we've given time off without pay and a letter of reprimand to a young writer who got information from a secretary and then characterized her as a "company spokesman." In a third, we fired a veteran writer for plagiarizing a feature story.

All the decisions were difficult. I've tried to approach these cases with three goals in mind: To be fair to the subjects and readers of our stories; to demonstrate the newspaper's commitment to ethical standards; and, where possible, to get the attention of and rehabilitate the staff members involved.

FRANK CAPERTON is executive editor of The Norfolk Virginian-Pilot *and* Ledger-Star.

When gambling came to our town

By Charles C. Reynolds

Stockbrokers, developers, and speculators were calling from such places as Los Angeles and London, asking how they could receive the *Atlantic City Press* on the day of publication.

It was 1979, and the *Press* was carrying almost daily accounts of potential casino developers, some legitimate, some marginally so, and some only grandiose schemers and dreamers. They were seeking and getting publicity in their efforts to cash in quickly on the financial success of Atlantic City's first casinos.

Stock prices in many of these companies fluctuated wildly, and the price changes often were influenced by announcements carried in the *Press.*

Our regular readers, concentrated in south Jersey, caught the fever. Many social conversations revolved around who had invested in what and how much money had been made.

Our staff members, not normally into the stock market, joined the game. Stock prices were discussed as never before in newsroom conversations. A handful of reporters and editors gathered around the rewrite desk late each afternoon as a local broker called in closing quotes for our listing of casino-related stocks.

It was an unhealthy situation. The continuing story was so pervasive that almost everybody on the news staff was involved to some degree. Any staffer who wrote a story, wrote a headline, wrote a caption, cropped a picture, or decided on the placement of a story or picture could theoretically use his or her position for personal gain.

I discussed the situation with two or three top editors and with our primary casino reporter. All of them assured me they held no casino-related stock, and neither they nor I could identify any instances in which news judgment was wrongly influenced.

Nevertheless, we agreed that some controls were needed. We also agreed that it would be unfair to staffers who were not directly involved in casino coverage to prohibit them from making a legitimate investment in a legal industry.

I obtained a copy of the *Wall Street Journal's* policy on stock transactions by employees. It proved helpful, but the *Journal* is far removed from the *Press.* Its guidelines did not provide a specific answer to our problem.

In the end, I sent a lengthy memo to each staff member outlining the dangers of our situation—from both legal and ethical standpoints—and directed each one to submit to me in confidence a listing of casino-related stock holdings. Any changes in holdings were to be reported within 24 hours. I said in the memo that I had never owned any casino-related stock and didn't intend to buy any.

My memo promised that staffers' holdings "will remain confidential with me unless I feel a need to discuss with other editors a staffer's specific performance on a specific news situation."

The response was excellent. Perhaps 20 percent of the staffers, not including any key editors, owned a few shares in casino-related companies. Many offered praise for the policy. I have not had to break the confidentiality of their replies.

Fortunately, there is no longer a problem. The frenzy of interest by developers has eased off, prices have stabilized and the *Press's* influence on prices is minimal.

Our eager subscribers in Los Angeles, London, and points beyond presumably are now getting their information from more traditional sources. And our staffers are back to normal, concentrating on giving local readers full coverage of newsworthy events.

CHARLES C. REYNOLDS is editor of The Atlantic City (N.J.) Press.

IV The need for compassion...

Old movies portray journalists as hard-drinking, hard-bitten rogues in search of sensational stories. New movies show packs of rapacious reporters preying on the victims of tragedy. Both images suggest a press insensitive to the needs of human beings, a press willing to trample on the rights of individuals on the way to a big story.

Most journalists will admit to a core of truth in both stereotypes. Too often, sensitivity is sacrificed to the pressure of deadline and the threat of competition. Journalists work hard to get the story right and to get it in the paper fast. The stories they write are often filled with morbid, disquieting news. A schoolteacher is accused of a sex crime, a woman gives birth to deformed twins, a young person is the victim of incest. Reporters have come to learn that a story can ruin a person's life—can even result in a suicide.

That is why journalists, at their best, never approach such stories in detached, callous ways. They consider the consequences of publication and recognize the need for compassion. More often than the public realizes, they temper journalism's traditional toughness with common decency.

It's our pain, too

By Steve Wilson

Being falsely accused of a crime has to be one of life's larger nightmares. It's more frightening when the charge is a sex crime. It's still worse when you're a public school teacher. And it's worse yet when your hometown newspaper decides the story belongs on the front page.

All of those things happened in 1978 to 55-year-old Charles Markham, an elementary music teacher in Lexington, Ky.

Markham was accused of indecent exposure by a 15-year-old girl, who said he exposed himself to her as she walked to school one morning. Police investigated the complaint before making the arrest, and they told a *Lexington Leader* reporter the charge was solid and others had seen him nude in his home.

It was the first time anyone in the newsroom could remember a sex charge placed against a school teacher in Lexington. That fact, plus the report from police that the case wasn't based solely on one girl's possible misperception or caprice, led us to run the story at the bottom of page one headlined, "Teacher here faces sex count."

We questioned ourselves at the time, asking whether we were being fair to a man who could be innocent. We wondered if we had properly balanced the story's news value with possible harm the story might do him. We wondered if running the story on page one unfairly implied that we were convinced of his guilt.

Our doubts were not diminished by several phone calls soon after the story was published from Markham's friends and neighbors. All spoke highly of him and said they couldn't believe Markham, who was married, could be guilty.

Two months later the case was tried in district court. After a brief deliberation, the jury found him not guilty.

49

After learning of the verdict, I remember two reactions: 1) The acquittal story would run the next day on page one, in the same spot as the original story, and 2) I wanted to speak with Charles Markham.

I reached him at home that evening. I told him I was sorry if the paper had made his ordeal more difficult. I said we regretted publishing the arrest story on the front page and would carry the acquittal story in the same place. His response was calm and courteous. He said he appreciated the call and the decision to report the jury's verdict prominently. He was looking forward to returning to his job. He asked only one thing: Could the word "teacher" be used in the headline to attract the same attention the arrest story received? I assured him it would.

I also wrote an editorial page column that day explaining why we were carrying the Markham story out front and describing the dilemma editors face when handling crime stories. We did what we could to remove the stigma of his accusation, knowing it could never be completely erased.

Editors will forever struggle to fulfill conflicting responsibilities to the public and to people accused of crimes they may not have committed. We can take the position that arrests are on the public record, that it's our job to report criminal activity and we can't become softhearted about someone who may be found innocent.

But we will be less than human if we can't feel some of the pain of a Charles Markham, and we will be less deserving of the public's respect if we don't consider that pain in making our decisions.

STEVE WILSON is assistant to the executive editor of The Detroit (Mich.) Free Press. From 1978 to 1982, he was editor of The Lexington (Ky.) Leader.

One city editor's baptism

By William Burleigh

I cut my journalistic eyeteeth on a tough, we-print-everything, no-exceptions-to-the-rule newspaper. Standards were standards and the mere thought of intentionally withholding news from print was anathema to all that was held sacred in the newsroom. I had seen the city editor spurn too many appeals for relaxation of the rules to believe there was any other way of doing things in the one true religion of professional journalism.

Eventually the city editor was promoted upstairs, but his orthodoxy, and the paper's, stayed in place when I inherited his chair.

It's been so long ago I can't recall the year or many of the details of the case that first cast in doubt the immutability of those time-tested, iron-clad standards. But I'll never forget the case itself.

We prided ourselves on printing in the daily public records section the disposition of every case in the municipal court. On deadline. No exceptions. Name, rank and serial number. The roll call offered rich fodder each evening for the town's gossip mill, although we cited much loftier reasons for the practice.

The phone call to the city desk framed the problem with utter clarity: If two court records, innocent enough by themselves, were allowed to appear, two young girls would be revealed as incest victims. I forget the precise connection but the point was, another news story had already been printed which would make the girls' identities clear to close readers of the records column.

I had heard my share of ingenious pleas for leaving records out of the paper. But this one was somehow different. I couldn't resort to the usual stonewalling or offer a highminded lecture about the ethics of printing *everything*.

No, on this one it was time for the young city editor to start asking himself some ethical questions. Did he really want to be the agent for branding these girls for life? If there was even a remote chance of causing such harm, no rule, however venerated, seemed worth that. Even if it did make him less of a macho city editor.

So I did something I had never done before. I took the city desk shears and whacked out the two court records before throwing the copy into the overnight basket.

As I recall, I never told anyone what I had done. I should, of course, have discussed it with the managing editor but I was afraid of the answer I would get. So I took it upon myself and felt guilty for doing so. I heard no more from the victims' family.

Later on we all came to grips more maturely with the ticklish questions of privacy and of not all news being fit to print. The pros and cons formed the agenda for stirring office debates. And the exceptions to the old rule grew.

But that was one city editor's baptism. He learned in the process that the job of editing yielded to few hard-and-fast rules and that a little dose of compassion wouldn't get him drummed out of the corps after all. Especially if he managed to keep it secret.

WILLIAM BURLEIGH is general editorial manager of Scripps-Howard.

Privilege isn't ethics

By Anthony E. Insolia

Most of the everyday problems of ethics that occur in a newsroom are really not that hard to deal with; the action required is usually plain to see.

The part of the ethical picture that is most troublesome is the search for consistency and equality. Why should we respond only to those individuals who request special treatment? How do we promulgate rules or guidelines when every situation has elements that make it somehow different?

Even as a young reporter for a small news agency in New York City, I knew it was wrong, after my boss agreed not to send the story to an upstate newspaper, to accept a gratuity from a relieved husband whose wife had been arrested for shoplifting. That was easy, although I have been bothered ever since by how readily my boss decided to spare this family the publicity we routinely gave to every out-of-town miscreant who ended up in the city courts.

Nor was it a tough decision when we discovered years ago that our hockey reporter was doubling as business agent for some of the players; he was fired. Equally obvious was the necessity of firing a staffer whose prose turned out to be much too similar to what had already appeared in another newspaper.

But what we all sometimes do is confuse privilege (in a legal sense) with ethical standards. Information reported by police or statements made at public gatherings is fair game, legally. But how necessary is the information to the story, even though we have the right to print it? For example, when the home of a wealthy family on Long Island's North Shore was burglarized, we reported that the family was on vacation and would not be back for a few weeks. The information was routinely obtained from police. Two weeks later the same house was burglarized again.

No one can say for sure that our initial report led to the second burglary. But in hindsight, it was easy to decide that the information about the house being empty for weeks to come had little value in the story and should have been excised.

I also agreed with another burglary victim who called from Florida to complain that our published detail about the installation of his burglar alarm system rendered the system useless and could easily have been omitted.

In another case, I feel we erred in omitting information. We routinely do not identify rape victims. However, in this case the state's high court upheld a charge against a man accused of having raped his wife. The editors that night decided that since we did not identify rape victims, we could not in this case identify the defendant. That rule is based on society's revulsion at this particular kind of crime, and the fact that the victim would suffer additionally through public shame. But this case was unusual, worthy of the attention of the high court, and in no way subjected the complainant to public embarrassment. The elements made this one vastly different from other rape stories.

When is someone's name, address, sexual preference, marital status, or other personal detail important to a story? These are the questions that are really hard to answer. Rules and guidelines, unfortunately, cover only the pat situations. The tough ones still rest where they should—with individual editors.

ANTHONY E. INSOLIA is editor of Newsday, Long Island, N.Y.

The Siamese twins case

By Robert H. Giles

Early in the afternoon of Sunday, March 27, 1983, a woman in a rural town 60 miles from Rochester, N.Y., called the metropolitan desk of the *Democrat and Chronicle.* The woman would not give her name. A police reporter, listening as she talked, began to scratch a few notes—"Siamese twins...connected at torso...parents from Steuben County."

The caller gave the family name, identified the doctor and said the twins had been moved to the intensive care nursery at Rochester's Strong Memorial Hospital.

The story was assigned to reporter Barbara Vancheri. Her first call was to hospital spokesman Milton Lederman at his home. Lederman confirmed that the twins were at the hospital, but he said he did not know the names of the parents.

Vancheri called the babies' physician, Dr. Donald Shapiro, who said the parents did not want any information released. Shapiro said he was concerned that the family would be hurt by the publicity.

Working with a telephone directory from Steuben County, Vancheri began calling the listings under the name she had been given.

On her first call, she reached the father of the twins. He wanted no publicity, he said, because the twins were not expected to live. Vancheri said she would pass his request on to her editors.

Later in the day, Dr. Shapiro told the reporter that "nothing would be gained by using the family's name."

Reporter Vancheri thought about the request and decided that she agreed with the father. "I wondered if it was an important element in the news story, particularly if the twins were joined in some almost-gruesome way and there were no plans to separate them."

About 6 p.m., Vancheri asked day editor Dianne Whitacre about the use of the name. Whitacre called Metro Editor Lou Ziegler, who was at home. Yes, he thought, the name should be published.

Later, Ziegler said, "I really didn't feel that this was a case where we would be adding to the family's grief by using the name." After all, the identity of the family would be known to the staff of the rural hospital where the twins were born, the staff of Strong Hospital and the ambulance company that brought them to Rochester. It would be impossible to keep the name a secret, he said.

Ziegler encouraged Whitacre to review his thoughts with the editors on the news desk who would be handling the copy for page one.

Those editors included Associate Editor Tom Flynn, News Editor Joette Riehle and Night Metro Editor Warren Watson. They worried about setting a precedent by agreeing to delete a name from a news story. They also suspected that television news broadcasts and regional newspapers would use the name. They wondered how they would feel if the *Democrat and Chronicle* was the only medium that did not identify the family.

Flynn reminded the editors that the twins' birth certificates would be available to other media the next day. It was likely that the parents' name would be used in a broadcast or another newspaper, he said.

The story was written with the names in the copy but no byline. Vancheri thought the family's request was fair and said she did not want her name on the story if the editors published the family name. She told the editors she was calling the family to let them know our decision. She did this as a courtesy, she said, so the family would not be surprised by the story in the Monday morning *Democrat and Chronicle*.

The father was upset and said he would call his lawyer. By 10 p.m., the lawyer was on the telephone, talking to Watson. Flynn consulted by telephone with Alice Lucan of Gannett's corporate legal staff. Lucan said the newspaper was within its rights to use the family name in the story. The family's lawyer called

56

the newsroom again at 10:30 p.m. and said the family would sue if they were identified in our news story. Flynn called me at home to explain the developments in the story, including the threat of a suit if we ran the name. I talked to Lucan to get a quick review of the questions of law that might arise.

My decision was to withhold the name. The pivotal question, it seemed to me, was whether there was any compelling reason for our readers to know the identity of the family. Beyond the normal practice of the newspaper to identify people in the news, was there something that would override the family's plea for privacy? On balance, I thought this was a story that called for compassion.

I called Flynn and told him we would not run the name. He pulled the page back and took the name out in time for the first edition deadline. He also phoned *USA TODAY,* which had been given the story by us, and convinced its editors to delete the name.

Eleven days later the twins died.

But their deaths did not mark the end of our coverage. Questions were raised about the twins' care and, under the Baby Doe Act, investigators were sent to Rochester.

The continuing story did not alter our decision not to publish the name. Nor, gratifyingly, did the *Times-Union,* the other daily newspaper in Rochester, regional newspapers, or the broadcast media identify the family.

ROBERT H. GILES is editor of The Rochester (N.Y.) Democrat and Chronicle-Times Union.

Compassion is a tough word

By Donald W. Gormley

Compassion. That's a tough word for a hard-bitten newsman to grasp. But there's a growing sense among readers of our newspapers that editors and reporters should show more compassion, so in our own best interest we'd better pay attention.

What do readers mean when they ask us to show more compassion? They mean don't put things in the paper that cause anguish. Don't show the bereaved the gory details of a fatal auto wreck. Don't picture people who are suffering through the pangs of losing a home or a loved one in a fire. In short, don't offend your readers unintentionally.

I think they are saying edit your papers with a consciousness that you can hurt people with no more reason than the fact that "it's a heck of a news picture."

Compassion is not the same as good taste. If a reader knows the person pictured in a very dramatic photograph, he may find it offensive. That's a sin against compassion. If he is offended whether he knows the person or not, the sin is probably one against good taste.

Let's be specific. Several years ago the *Spokesman-Review* ran a page one photo of a young woman attorney in the grasp of a couple of police officers. She had run her car into the Spokane River, crawled out safely, and had time to light a cigaret before emergency vehicles and a *Spokesman-Review* photographer arrived on the scene. When the officers solicitously tried to help her, or question her, she resisted their efforts and was photographed. The officers wound up charging her with driving while intoxicated.

The most interesting part of the story came to light a little later in the office. The driver was identified as Julie Twyford, a defense attorney for a man

58

who had been arrested as the notorious "South Hill rapist," convicted of four rapes in a dramatic and well-covered trial in Spokane and who had on that very day been sentenced to life plus 75 years in the penitentiary. Suddenly we had a fresh, gripping news picture to go with a very dramatic story—a definition of ecstasy for the managing editor of an a.m. who had already seen the story published in the competing afternoon paper. We played it as we saw it. Compassion for Julie Twyford was not high in our consciousness. It was a heck of a news picture, and it got the big play.

Within a couple of hours of delivery of the paper, a barrage of phone calls tied up the newsroom. The next day a flood of mail began to pour in. Julie Twyford had a lot of friends, and they were incensed at our insensitivity. How could we, they demanded, be so eager to destroy a fine young woman's career and reputation? How could we be so unfeeling, so cruel, so beastly? They weren't just asking rhetorical questions, either. They wanted answers. They were asking valid questions, ones that dealt as much with our ethics as with their anger. Spokane is a medium-sized community, in which a lot of people know a lot of other people, and we had distressed a lot of them. In a big city, perhaps the photo would not have had such impact. Maybe editors in smaller communities can't use the same standards as those on the big metros.

Was use of the picture in the *Spokesman-Review* justified on the basis of news value alone? I submit that it was. Is news value alone a justification for running the picture? Two years ago I didn't have a doubt. Today I'm not so sure.

DONALD W. GORMLEY is general manager of The Spokane (Wash.) Spokesman-Review.

The threat of suicide

By Ray Moscowitz

Shortly before 10 o'clock on a routine Monday morning, City Editor Debi Warlaumont told me that Joyce Castle, a black assistant principal of a Michigan City high school, had been arrested Sunday and charged with shoplifting.

"We're going with a separate story, rather than putting it in the police roundup," Warlaumont said. "We can't treat it as a routine shoplifting item when someone as well known as she—a person who's a role-model—gets picked up and charged."

I agreed without hesitation.

When Jerry Pearson, our only black reporter, heard about the arrest, he took great interest. Pearson covered education; he knew Castle well.

He told Warlaumont he was going to Castle's office to see if the theft had actually occurred. If so, he wanted to explain why it had to be reported.

As Castle talked about her shame, she said she would commit suicide if her name appeared in the *News-Dispatch*. Her career had suffered a tremendous blow.

It was no ordinary career. She had earned a well-deserved reputation as an educator who handled discipline and attendance problems well.

After talking to Pearson for about 10 minutes, Castle suddenly got up from her desk, grabbed her coat and left.

Pearson returned to the office, shaken. He did not know where Castle had gone. All he could talk about was her deep depression and suicide threat.

Would she really commit suicide if her name and arrest appeared in the newspaper? Yes, Pearson was convinced. Managing Editor Leo Morris, Warlaumont, and I decided to hold the story until we could get more information.

I called the high school and asked for Castle. I was told that she had gone home for the day, ill.

Suicide threats were not new to me. Years earlier, at an other small-town newspaper, a woman arrested for shoplifting walked into the newsroom and made the threat to the night editor. He called me at home. In turn, I called a county official I trusted. Did he know the woman well? Yes. Would she follow through on her threat? Yes. I wasn't about to have blood on my hands. The public record isn't sacred; the purists be damned. I called the night editor and told him to leave the arrest out; he was aghast. (A few months later the woman committed suicide over another matter. She had a history of mental problems, I learned.)

Now, with Joyce Castle, I decided, again, that I would not have blood on my hands.

I was asked, "What if WIMS (the local radio station) reports it on its noon news and we don't have it in that day's paper?" I couldn't answer.

I asked Pearson if he knew where Castle lived. He did. I sent him there and told him to call me by 11:30.

Pearson checked in. Castle was home in bed, under sedation, with two friends standing watch. They had heard the suicide "rumor" too. That took any doubt out of my mind.

But what about the radio station?

We turned on the noon news. No mention of Castle.

Later in the day, we contacted school officials. Castle's immediate supervisor, the principal, had not heard about her arrest, nor had the school superintendent. The next day, having checked with police, the school superintendent said he had no choice but to suspend her until the case went through the judicial process.

We could not, of course, ignore the story forever, but decided we would not print until we were sure Castle was emotionally well. A week went by, and calls to the paper began as word of the arrest spread around our town of 37,000. We were called, among other epithets, nigger-lovers.

Finally, we learned that Castle had recovered and planned to resign at the next school board meeting.

I decided we would report her resignation and the reasons for it as part of the general school board story. A sidebar on her resignation, I felt, was not necessary and could possibly cause her additional emotional harm.

In our school board story, 20 days after the shoplifting arrest, we reported Castle's resignation in her own words: "For various reasons—illness being the most important—I find it necessary to relocate...." We then reported that she had been charged with shoplifting on March 28. We reported that store personnel told police she put a $15 ham in a handbag and did not pay for it at the checkout counter. We reported that the prosecutor would handle the case under deferred prosecution, in which Castle would be assigned 20 to 30 days of community service "in her field of expertise." We also reported that the theft incident was not discussed during the board meeting.

The black community—about 18 percent of Michigan City—reacted with great anger, arguing that the shoplifting incident should never have been reported. On the other hand, some in the white community accused us of a coverup.

I would do the same thing again—and, I like to think, even if the radio had carried the story. We reported the facts, albeit late, of an incident involving a prominent member of our community. At the same time, we did not contribute to the possible suicide of a human being.

RAY MOSCOWITZ is editor of The Michigan City (Ind.) News Dispatch.

V ...And the need to publish

The watchdog function of the press impels journalists to expose political corruption and abuses of power. In cases of crime, ineptitude, or hypocrisy which threaten the public good, the need to publish becomes paramount. Newspapers print such information so that citizens in a democracy can make important decisions on issues that affect their welfare.

In such cases, journalists think of themselves as the eyes and ears of the voter, the champion of the oppressed, the voice of the voiceless. They assume adversarial relationships to powerful institutions, sometimes at great cost. Subscribers cancel. Advertisers move to a competitor. Letters and phone calls threaten violence. In the ideal world, the virtuous editor persists in a search for the truth.

Some journalists recognize the dangers of an unrelenting adversarial posture by the press. It has been suggested that in a news atmosphere poisoned by negativism and cynicism, all institutions come into question, including the press itself. The press needs its power to uncover the corruption of power. But to best exercise its constitutional prerogatives, the press must not abuse its own power.

Keeping good enemies

By John Strohmeyer

An editor in a community of our size is generally distinguished by the friends he keeps and the enemies he develops. I found early in life that keeping good friends was harder than keeping good enemies.

Raymond C. Dietz was one of my more durable friends, not in a social sense but in a more important way. Early in my career he commended our editorials on the mess in city government, and then he personally did something about it.

In the late 1950s, he was in the forefront of the move to replace the city's outdated commission form of government. He encouraged "Action in Practical Politics" courses for civic leaders, enrolling himself. Then, in the 1960s, he became a candidate on a council ticket that swept the corruption-ridden administration out of city hall.

Dietz was a good councilman, serving two terms and helping the city through a renaissance that would give us a new city center, a new library, and honest government. Then he left for what should have been a happy retirement.

It was shocking, therefore, to learn one day in September 1982 that ex-councilman Dietz was seriously injured and arrested for drunken driving after a car he was apparently driving rammed a light pole.

Something went badly awry in our judicial system when his case came before a magistrate. The drunken driving charge was dismissed in a way that left police and the public amazed.

A witness who ran across the street to pull Dietz from behind the steering wheel was not permitted to testify, except to answer one question: Did he see the car actually crash? When he answered "No," he was not asked what he did see. It then became academic that police had results of a blood test which registered

Dietz's alcohol content at .24 of a percent. A reading of .10 is all that is needed for conviction.

The district attorney's office, which we had strongly criticized in the past for hypocritical law enforcement, botched the case. Further, an accused drunken driver was let off unpunished at a time when a fever for tough enforcement of drunk driving laws was sweeping the state.

The Dietz case underscored what we had been saying about the district attorney's office. It also affirmed our editorial position that coddling drunk drivers was responsible for a growing danger for innocent people on the road.

Yet, Dietz had hurt no one but himself and a light pole. He was at that moment lying bruised and battered in a hospital bed. The publicity about the accident and arrest had already tarnished an upstanding career. Hadn't he suffered enough? Wouldn't the total interest be served if we simply went on to other editorial subjects and let the Dietz case alone?

The painful decision was to pursue the issue. On Nov. 2, 1982, an editorial, titled "Another Assault on Even Justice," scored the prosecution, stating "We are left to ponder one more example of uneven justice, one more hypocrisy in drunk driving prosecutions, and one more reason to be cynical about the district attorney's capacity for courageous law enforcement."

The editorial caused such heat that the district attorney decided to rearrest Dietz, blaming us for it. "The intentional prejudice of the public by the press makes it necessary to appeal to the court for the rearrest," he said.

However, before the rearrest case could be heard, Dietz died in St. Luke's Hospital.

Did our editorial decision hasten Dietz's death? Did we place an opportunity to prove an editorial point above consideration of the impact it might have on the health of an individual who had served his city— and us—so well? Would I make the same decision if faced with it again?

I asked myself all those questions and concluded that we had done the proper thing. Had we not challenged the district attorney, a terrible standard of prosecution ineptness would have been deemed acceptable.

The D.A. is still an enemy, and I suspect we might be on a similar Dietz family list. I ease that thought only by telling myself that we fought not against Dietz but for a public principle. I believe it was an editorial stand true to the ones that Dietz supported us on way back when.

JOHN STROHMEYER is vice president and editor of The Bethlehem (Pa.) Globe-Times.

Integration in Oak Ridge

By Dick Smyser

When the first stirrings of integration moved through the South in the late 1950s, U.S. Atomic Energy Commission officials insisted that Oak Ridge housing wasn't segregated.

Neither was the municipal swimming pool in this then still very young and federally owned and operated community. (Oak Ridge was built by the Manhattan Engineering District during World War II to house workers in the top secret atomic bomb project.)

It was just, said the AEC, that no blacks had ever chosen to rent houses or apartments in other than the Scarboro Community, the black ghetto carefully constructed a quarter mile from the rest of the community. Nor had any black sought admission to the swimming pool, the same federal officials insisted, before one finally did in 1955—and was admitted, although with considerable unpleasantness.

But now private home ownership had come to the city, and a young black biologist and his wife with a toddler decided that they did want to live other than in Scarboro.

The word that they would move into a small two-bedroom home in one of Oak Ridge's all-white neighborhoods spread quickly.

When the *Oak Ridger* began making inquiries, the reaction was immediate.

A delegation from a citizens' group "working quietly" toward integration came to our office. If we printed anything, the couple would most surely be harassed, they said. The individual selling the house might be pressured not to sell. The house might be bombed or burned.

A highly respected clergyman (respected by the newspaper, too) argued most strenuously against any sort of news report:

- Had we put it in the paper when the editor moved into his house?
- If we favored integration—and we did, and had said so editorially numerous times—why would we want to do anything to interfere with this important step?

There was another reaction to the rumors, which now had it that not just this family but as many as eight or ten black families might be planning to move into the same neighborhood: Why was the newspaper hushing all this up? (Those calling to make this complaint used terms other than "black families.")

We listened, yet knew that we must print. But we would not do so on the basis only of plans. Once the family was in the house, however, it was news.

When they did move in, we called the family promptly. They were not happy—said they feared for their safety. We argued that their occupancy of the house was no secret—could not be a secret. And the rumor mill was alive with distorted reports. But they still objected strongly, although they did give the information we sought.

How to play the story?

A cold news call said as the lead story, maybe even a banner head. (The *Oak Ridger's* emphasis is strongly on local news.) Some of those pleading with us not to run the story had suggested that, if we absolutely did have to publish, we should run only a paragraph or two buried back inside. This would answer those who accused us of suppression but might be less likely "to get everyone all upset."

We used the story halfway down page one with a headline alluding to a housing milestone rather than a racial precedent.

We worked very hard on that story—rethought each word. But we worked equally hard to see that it was clear and complete, that it would counter all rumors with facts, and that it would avoid, to the extent possible, emotionalism.

Explicit but not exploitative–that was our objective.

Within days after the story ran, the family called to say that while they had had some anxious moments, the larger effect was one of clearing the air. Some of the citizens' group that had urged us so strongly not to print also conceded that we had done the right thing.

DICK SMYSER is editor of The Oak Ridge (Tenn.) Oak Ridger.

Undercover at Big Nell's

By A. N. Romm

"You won't believe this," the Newburgh bureau chief said, as he spread a map of a proposed urban renewal project on my desk. "They're going to tear down the old Dutch Reformed Church, while just 50 feet away they're making Big Nell's and other property eligible for restoration funds."

"But we've quoted the police chief as saying Big Nell's is closed—out of business," I countered.

"I'll find out," said the dauntless reporter.

"Okay," I said. "But if you go inside, for God's sake don't tell anyone you work for the *Record.*" I felt not a twinge of sensitivity to the question of journalistic ethics on concealed identity (I hadn't *directly* ordered that) or commission of a misdemeanor (I certainly hadn't directed a reporter to commit the infraction of soliciting a prostitute's services).

He and an equally dauntless staffer did enter Newburgh's legendary house of prostitution that very night. To nail down the story, each (married) young reporter went upstairs with a girl. Only one said he fully played out his role as client.

On the next cycle, we cheerfully published the urban renewal expose', with salty sidebar material, to the extreme discomfiture of the Newburgh police and other officials. The urban renewal decision was reversed. The church was saved and became a historic landmark. Big Nell's wasn't renovated at taxpayer's expense.

With a flourish, I countersigned the most unusual expense voucher ever submitted to me.

Big Nell's closed shop for a few weeks but reopened in time for state police to raid and padlock the establishment. The district attorney, convinced that my reporters' testimony was needed to buttress that of the state troopers, who hadn't caught anyone in the act, subpoenaed the reporters. The state shield law was no protection; confidentiality had been neither promised or implied. The D.A.'s examination was a piece of cake, but cross examination of the reporters was withering and embarrassing.

I myself was called as a hostile witness for Big Nell's defense.

"Is it your practice," asked Big Nell's counsel, "to command reporters to conceal their identity and violate the law in search of a story?"

"No," I answered. "My concern was to protect them from harm. I gave no specific orders."

After an hour of verbal sparring, the judge mercifully called a halt to the interrogation.

The jury convicted Big Nell. The judge sentenced the aging madame to a year in jail after she refused his offer of probation if she would but identify her municipal protectors.

My post-conviction editorial said in part: "We aren't in the business of committing crimes or condoning commission of crimes...but we will not flinch...from our watchdog role in the public interest. Even if our investigation takes us into gambling dens (or) to the center of narcotics traffic, where our men might buy some stuff so as not to destroy their camouflage. And even if it takes us inside a bordello, where our men might have to pay their dues to determine if men and women are teaming up to play gin rummy in upstairs rooms—or something else."

How do I feel today?

I regret only that we didn't fight vigorously the subpoenas that turned the reporters into prosecution witnesses. A newspaper should not be seen as a willing tool of the establishment.

On the issue of committing an infraction in pursuit of a story—the point Prof. Arthur Miller and his associates dwell on with gusto in their press/bar hypotheticals—I still have no problem. Let the court and the court of public opinion judge our actions on a case-by-case basis.

On the basis of concealing identity, by omission or commission, my editorial point holds. I'll go one step further:

If the otherwise valuable codes of ethics newspapers are shaping or reshaping bar us in certain investigations from assuming the identity of a customer, then the watchdog becomes a pussycat.

A. N. ROMM is director of news quality and training for Ottaway Newspapers and is former editor of The Middletown (N.Y) Times Herald-Record.

But isn't football sacred?

By William J. Woestendiek

It was a tough and scary decision, but it proved to be the right one.

When I suggested to our staff at the *Arizona Daily Star* that we ought to check out the University of Arizona football program because of some of the unsavory things that seemed to be going on at rival Arizona State University, I had no idea where it would lead. I simply presumed that, since it was part of the same state system, the U. of A. might have its own recruiting problems.

When reporters Clark Hallas and Bob Lowe started poring through records, they found, among other strange items, expense vouchers for hotel bills listing only the last name and first initial of the room occupants. These people were allegedly potential football recruits, and the expenses had been approved by coach Tony Mason.

When the "recruits" turned out to be women, we ran the story, and the roof fell in. As our reporters began an intensive investigation of every aspect of the football program, I became the target of a vicious campaign by the community.

In more than 35 years in the business, I have never been vilified or threatened more. And this time the threats and the anger came not from the gun nuts or religious fanatics but from business leaders, wealthy alumni, the president of the university and other prominent citizens.

Business leaders met with me at a secret breakfast to tell me that we could not continue with this investigation because we would be destroying not only a great football program but a great university and a coach and his family. Automobile dealers threatened to boycott us—and eventually did. I was told that I was going to be run out of town and received letters threatening harm to my family.

74

The investigation continued and developed additional evidence of expense account cheating, of money being given players and of players being paid by the city for work they didn't do.

But after the first story, I held off publishing anything else. Despite reportorial pressure, it was my feeling that we should give the coach and the athletic director an opportunity to respond to some of these charges. I also wanted to be absolutely sure that we did not unfairly "ruin a program or a family." Other media in the city, including the television stations and the sports department of the opposition newspaper, ripped us unmercifully.

To prove our good faith, I postponed publication of any further stories until after the Fiesta Bowl game, in which the University of Arizona was to play, so that we could not be accused of destroying team morale. Coach Mason agreed to meet with us to answer the charges after the bowl game. When he failed to do so, I decided to go with everything we had, including details on a fake airline ticket scam that Mason and his other coaches were using to get money for trips they never took. Eventually Mason was forced to resign and was charged with numerous felonies, the athletic director departed, and the university was placed on probation by the NCAA.

A footnote: The *Arizona Daily Star* won the Pulitzer Prize for the investigation.

WILLIAM J. WOESTENDIEK is editorial director of The Cleveland (Ohio) Plain Dealer.

The reality of suicide

By Watson Sims

He was a prominent businessman and held a major post in county government. He had asked to visit and chat about a new project, but now he leaned back and changed the subject.

"You know, I'm human, too," he said. "I can make mistakes."

Browsing in K-Mart Saturday, he had picked up screws and washers for a household chore, put them in his pocket and forgotten to pay. He was caught at the door and charged with shoplifting.

"It's ridiculous," he said. "I am a wealthy man. If I am going to steal, it will not be for two dollars."

This man charged with shoplifting! I was astounded. Why didn't he simply explain things to the store manager?

"He doesn't like me. It's personal. I'm going to fight it, of course, but you've got to keep it out of the paper."

But we couldn't do that. We wouldn't blow the story up, but we could not cover it up.

"Do you mean you carry a story every time Tom, Dick, or Harry is caught in something this small?"

But he was not Tom, Dick, or Harry. He was a public servant and the public had a right to know about any problem he had with the law. This right was not mine to give away; he had asked for something I did not possess.

We were both upset and unhappy when he left my office.

The case came to trial. He was found guilty and placed on probation. We published three inches under a one-column headline on an inside page.

Three days later I had an electrifying telephone call: The man had committed suicide. There was a note that police would not release.

76

Had we been wrong to publish the story?

On sleepless nights, the question ran back and forth through my mind.

Must a newspaper inform the public whenever an official is in trouble with the law? Is there an exception to every rule? Is it proper that whenever anyone is wounded, by mistake, misfortune, or malfeasance, the media's telling of the event becomes part of the consequences? Should editors be concerned with mercy as well as accuracy?

The questions stung, but I could find only one answer: An editor knows if a story belongs in his paper, and if it belongs, it must be published.

Two events helped lift some of my burden of conscience. One was learning from the chief of police that the suicide note referred to several problems but made no mention of the shoplifting incident. The other was a chance encounter with the manager of K-Mart.

"I didn't want to have him arrested but I had no choice," the manager told me. "He had stolen things over and over again, and our employees knew about it. I had warned him it had to stop."

Suddenly I realized that editors are by no means the only people who must agonize over the need to take unpleasant positions in the line of duty. It was a conclusion to remember as other years brought other painful decisions to one editor's door.

WATSON SIMS is editor of The New Brunswick (N.J.) Home News.

VI When in Rome...

American editors strongly defend the position that a free press can help a society towards more democratic institutions and a higher standard of living for its people. Others argue in favor of a more controlled system of information, one which tends to support fragile governments and struggling economies.

Unfortunately, many societies lack a free press and suppress the open expression of ideas. In many cases, the only reliable information about totalitarian governments comes from Western reporters working for Western news organizations.

In some circumstances, journalists are torn between the desire to print the truth and the knowledge of the terrible consequences of publication for a news source. In an environment hostile to press freedom, a journalist may feel the need to adjust his behavior, to fight against his normal instincts, to protect an innocent abroad.

The need to protect sources, especially vulnerable ones, exists for journalists in all cultures and environments. Too often, whistle-blowers are punished for their actions.

It was funny, but...

By Seymour Topping

As a young reporter covering the war in French Indochina in 1958 for The Associated Press, I made a damaging blunder that ingrained in me a lasting guideline for ethical behavior. I had traveled from my base in Saigon to Phnom Penh, where Norodom Sihanouk then reigned as king of Cambodia. In the American legation, huge chuckles were resounding about a series of cable exchanges between King Sihanouk and President Truman.

The King, grateful for United States aid, had informed the President that he was bestowing the gift of an elephant on the White House. Seeing this gift as a veritable white elephant, the White House was politely trying to decline the offer, especially when it became known that a Cambodian mahout would have to accompany the beast to Washington. But consideration of the sensitivities of the Cambodian monarch finally prevailed, and the unwanted elephant was soon aboard ship en route to the United States. Unexpectedly, and to the vast relief of the White House, the elephant succumbed, apparently to seasickness, and was buried in the Pacific.

All of this was detailed in an extended exchange of cables between the legation and the State Department. A senior official of the legation, pleased to tell of this comic relief amid the grimness of civil war, turned copies of the cables over to me. There seemed no better way for me to report the story than simply to carry the texts of the cables in sequence. That they were couched in protocolese made the elephant affair even more hilarious. AP Features devoted a full page to my story, which was carried in hundreds of newspapers. It was one of the best played features of the year, and many congratulatory messages followed.

81

But then came the shocker. King Sihanouk protested to President Truman. The White House scolded the State Department. And the Department landed in all fury on the legation in Phnom Penh. My friendly official at the legation confessed and was reprimanded. His career no doubt had suffered a setback.

When I learned of this consequence of my scoop, I anguished over the damages done to my source. He had provided me with copies of the cables without ground rules, assuming, I suppose, that an unprovocative tale of the elephant contretemps without sourcing would appear one day. Publication of the texts of the cables, which were classified, although in a low category, came as a surprise to him. It had never occurred to me that this would be the aftermath of a funny story from a remote gingerbread capital. My mea culpa to my source's immediate boss did little good, but a subsequent conversation with an assistant secretary of state in Washington mitigated the reprimand in his personnel file.

As for my lesson, never again would I write a sensitive story without carefully weighing whether I had been fair to my sources. Certainly, the first journalistic obligation is to the reader, particularly if the public interest is involved. But sources should not only be quoted accurately and in perspective, but also protected if circumstances require. Frankness, rather than manipulation, should be the rule in obtaining information from the innocent and the naive.

SEYMOUR TOPPING is managing editor of The New York Times.

Meanwhile, back in Russia...

By Loren Ghiglione

The big ethical issues—the ones that invite boycotts and make textbooks—don't seem to bother me as much as the small ones.

Sergei Vishnevsky, *Pravda* columnist on issues of war and peace, had visited my home in Southbridge, Mass., following a conference in New Hampshire. I had visited his home in Moscow during a second Soviet-U.S. conference. We had talked frankly about our work and our lives.

I tried to explain the four faces of this complex man: the bon vivant in love with perpetual loquacity, the official spokesman for the Communist Party, the ulcer-ridden victim and the schizophrenic walking the tightrope between telling the truth and fudging it in accordance with the Soviet line.

At one point in his U.S. visit, for instance, he told me, "You live better than I do." I noted the irony of such an admission from a columnist for *Pravda*, a Communist Party organ that enjoys portraying the United States as a land of nonopportunity and unemployment.

I reported Vishnevsky's comment. It supported my point that he, to maintain his sources and his self-respect, lets Westerners know he is aware of the truth even if he will not—or cannot—print it.

Besides, Vishnevsky is part of a system of doublespeak that deserved to be described in detail by someone on the receiving end. At worst, it seemed, I was forcing Vishnevsky to live with his own words.

Then I began to second-guess myself. How would Soviet officials view Vishnevsky's admission?

I read a report by Raymond Garthoff, a senior fellow at the Brookings Institution, who wrote, "In Moscow this is no time (for Soviets) to seem to be 'soft on the Americans.' "

I telephoned a U.S. correspondent formerly stationed in Moscow. He carefully avoided giving advice. But he questioned whether I should have printed Vishnevsky's comment and other remarks. "They could get him in big trouble."

In the Soviet Union, a statement of truth can become a ticket to professional oblivion.

If I could rewrite that profile today, I would eliminate Vishnevsky's statement. My stomach tells me I made a mistake.

An American journalist abroad needs to heed the U.S. ethical standards he knows and respects but he also needs to learn the host country's standards, even if he abhors them. And he needs to remember when compassion is as important as the truth.

LOREN GHIGLIONE is the editor of The Southbridge, (Mass.) News.

VII A case for restraint

Readers complain that editors print sensational stories to make money. If they could attend a news meeting or overhear conversations between reporters and editors, they might be surprised how often the case is made for restraint.

Readers do not know what information is left out of the paper: grisly details about murders and traffic fatalities; information about the victims of rape or incest; gossip about the personal lives of public figures; stories of questionable taste which no one would want to read over breakfast.

Paragraphs are deleted, photos are cropped, entire stories are withheld, all because editors realize that readers have a right *not* to know certain information, especially in a family newspaper.

The cost of restraint is sometimes as high as the cost of publication: loss of revenue, frustration and low morale. But one test of an ethical newspaper is whether it must act, on occasion, against its obvious or convenient self interest for some high purpose. In the long run, readers will respect and support a publication that can be both aggressive in the pursuit of the truth and responsible in its handling of sensitive information.

Sticking with named sources

By Alex S. Jones

The distraught father shot himself, but in the stomach instead of the heart where he had intended. When a deputy sheriff arrived, he burbled in his pain: "Help my son."

The son, a junior loan officer at a local bank, had confessed to his father the day before that he had made a series of fraudulent loans in order to help finance a big marijuana buy in Colombia. He told his story to state attorneys who quickly turned the case over to the FBI, and an investigation began.

Among law enforcement people, rumors began to bubble up. The rumor was that "someone big, someone who will surprise you" had master-minded a large scale marijuana conspiracy. Inquiries turned up the name of a former assistant attorney general, now in a private law practice with his wife.

Although we learned what was going on fairly early in the investigation, we did not publish what we knew. To do so would have required our using unnamed sources, since there was no official confirmation of any aspect of the investigation.

We had occasionally published stories using unnamed sources in the past, but we avoided doing so whenever possible, and we were especially careful when a person's life and reputation were at stake. In this case, to print such an allegation would destroy the man's reputation without his ever being charged with a crime.

Luckily for us, the man under investigation was known to be no friend of the newspaper.

The investigation was conducted in secrecy. One week before a federal grand jury was to hear the evidence, a rival newspaper from a town 40 miles away broke the story under banner headlines.

We had considered this possibility, and had determined that we would stick with our policy and print only what information we could confirm.

It was a costly decision.

Our rival editor, seeing that we were not going to print material which neither he nor we could confirm, launched a blitzkrieg.

Story upon story poured out, all attributed to unnamed sources.

Carloads of kids were shuttled 40 miles to sell newspapers on the street—including at every entrance to our plant. More than a hundred radio spots were purchased, all suggesting that we were engaged in a cover-up, and that only our rival would tell what "prominent local people" were involved in the drug conspiracy.

Coin machines selling the opposition newspaper appeared overnight. The *Sun's* penetration of its market is first in Tennessee and 16th in the country, and the opposition had never been able to gain a foothold in the past. But with this new opportunity, teams of salesmen hit our neighborhoods offering introductory offers. It was a circulation disaster. In addition, even our most loyal customers did not understand our position. Why were we not printing the names? Whom were we protecting? Were we covering up for the big shots?

Staff morale was on the floor, and character assassination was rampant. The town was whipped into hysteria, and the opposition's newspapers were selling like hotcakes.

The pressure, in short, was enormous.

The reputations we had set out to protect until and unless indictments were forthcoming had been shattered. The opposition's news stories had named them, and they were common currency.

Was there any reason not to run with the ball and print all we knew, using unnamed sources like our rivals?

And what about the hysteria? Surely it would calm the town to be told who was involved and who was not.

On the other hand, I felt that what was happening was wrong, and I especially resented the insinuation by our rival newspaper that we were engaged in a coverup. Our position had been stated in a front page editorial in which we had said flatly that it was wrong to destroy a person's reputation based on information which could not be confirmed, unless there was reason to think that justice was not going to be done. In this case, the law enforcement apparatus was working well.

Since the reputations were no longer at stake, the issue became a murky one of principle.

As information, the names were old news. The issue now was whether or not we would violate our previously stated position.

My decision was that the unconfirmed names would not be printed until the people were indicted. So we scrambled like hell to get confirmed information. A local Colombian woman became our investigative reporter, and she spent hours on the telephone to Colombia. We broke several stories on how the plot had faltered. As it turned out, the whole conspiracy had become a farcical failure. The conspirators ran out of gas flying to Colombia, landed at a Colombian Air Force base, and were immediately arrested. They never saw a leaf of marijuana.

The sheriff also confirmed that two of his deputies were under investigation, and we published that story, using named sources.

The grand jury did not return indictments at its first meeting, and we had to wait several more weeks for it to do so.

On the day the indictments came down, we delayed our press start for four hours to be first—and complete—with the story.

It is terrible to watch customers flock to a competitor's newspaper and to fight with one hand tied behind one's back.

We may have lost some subscribers doing what we did. Still, some who were screaming the loudest have since made a point of apologizing, telling us that we were right and thanking us for handling it as we did.

Overall, I feel we gained in stature. But all of us who were involved look back at those days and shudder.

ALEX S. JONES is a correspondent for The New York Times and is the former editor of The Greenville (Tenn.) Sun.

Brutal murder, sober restraint

By Susan Miller

When Eric Johnson returned home the afternoon of Friday, April 9, 1983, he found his wife, Kathleen, methodically stabbing the already dead bodies of their two young sons. Eric screamed for Kathy to stop. She ignored him. When police arrived at the University of Illinois married student housing complex, they had to restrain the slightly built, frecklefaced young woman.

Coverage of the case posed extraordinary questions about privacy, taste, journalistic independence and to what extent a news medium should try to help a community to cope with tragedy.

Kathleen Johnson, 22, had not only stabbed to death 3-year-old Jeremiah and 2-year-old Mike, but had decapitated and disemboweled her elder son. A veteran officer called it the most awful thing he'd ever seen.

Through sheer coincidence, the *News-Gazette* had taken a photo of the family four months earlier—making Christmas cookies. I chose to have the photographer isolate a mug shot of each of the children from his negatives, for use on page one. I thought shots of the victims were an important element to the story. A sidebar to our main story quoted stunned neighbors who knew Kathy Johnson as an attentive, devoted mother.

For our Sunday morning paper we ran a straightforward second-day lead: Kathy Johnson would be charged with murder. Several questions cried out to be answered: Who is Kathy Johnson? What is she like? What triggered the violence?

And what about Eric? We had only the barest of details about both. He was local, the son of a University of Illinois professor, but we couldn't find anyone who had grown up with him. She had been a high school honor student in Peoria. Neighbors said they were a typical student family, outwardly wholesome, churchgoing.

In an effort to convey what we had been told about Kathy and Eric, I decided to run the full-frame file photo of the family making Christmas cookies. More than anything we could have written at that point, it conveyed what her friends knew of Kathy Johnson: She hovers protectively behind the two toddlers as they cut cookie dough, flanked by her equally attentive husband.

We were roundly criticized for using that photo. Readers called us insensitive to the family's grief. Later, however, we learned that the family life had not been idyllic. Kathy Johnson had a boyfriend, whose attentions she may have encouraged only to make her husband jealous. She apparently regarded Eric as insensitive and domineering. She was shy, immature, insecure, all of which came out at the trial. But knowing only what we knew then, trying to convey to a shocked and even frightened community the "normalness" of the Johnson family, if I had it to do over again, I still would run that photo.

On Sunday afternoon Kathy Johnson was charged with murder during an unusual hearing held inside the mental health center where she was being held. We had the only reporter, Jim Dey, on the scene—in part because he was the only one able to find out where and when it would take place. The presiding judge, Robert Steigmann, agreed to allow him to attend because he trusted Dey not to sensationalize the story.

Steigmann did not expect us to pool the story with other media. He feared other reporters—especially TV crews—would turn the hearing into a circus.

On Monday, we led with the results of the Sunday hearing, used a file headshot of Kathy, eyes downcast, and reported she had a history of mental illness, and had attempted to take her own life Sunday

Was that relevant? I think so. It was an attempt to explain how such a crime could have occurred. Many people had considered Kathy a model parent.

92

Neighbors had spent the weekend in a state of shock, trying to explain the murders to their own children, wondering if they themselves were capable of similar actions.

Our coverage of the trial four months later included some testimony on the decapitation, the disemboweling, the boyfriend, the Johnsons' disagreements. We played it on page 3, with other local news. The acquittal by reason of insanity made page one. Radio and television were much less restrained in documenting the gory details that came out during the trial, but by then, the shock in the community had subsided and many of the grim details had already leaked out.

With the reservation that our initial coverage may have been too sympathetic to Kathy Johnson, I remain comfortable with what we did.

SUSAN MILLER is executive editor of The Champaign-Urbana (Ill.) News-Gazette

Who ever told you ethics would be easy?

Few things produce as much anxiety for some journalists as the discussion of newspaper ethics. Ethics smacks of censorship, either imposed by a government agency or by peers. Neither form goes over well in a field whose practitioners pride themselves on being independent, autonomous and beholden to no one.

Speak of ethics and the journalist envisions an ethereal system full of rigid rules, unbreakable prescriptions and abstract codes. Journalists are more likely to put their moral faith in intuition and gut feelings rather than in the ornate theoretical constructions of moral philosophers or theologians.

Nevertheless, just like the character in Moliere's play who was delighted to learn that she had been speaking prose all her life, it may come as a surprise to those who read these cases to learn that, whether they are aware of it or not, journalists engage in ethical thinking throughout their professional lives.

Value judgments are at the heart of the practice of journalism. While it may seem grandiose to label decisions about how many inches a story will receive or whether someone's name will be omitted from a particular item as ethical, they are certainly no less so than the agonizing decisions about weightier matters of fairness, balance and objectivity. Only the familiarity of these everyday choices within the world of journalism disguises their ethical content.

The discussions in the various cases reveal another and more important fact about ethics and journalism. Each case is both difficult and unique. No simple moral rule of thumb satisfactorily handles all of them. But those who read these cases should not lose sight of the ethical forest for all of the many moral trees that are described.

A number of prescriptions, considerations and indeed, moral rules form a constant background for the case discussions. In each case the contributors reveal

95